'HOW NOT TO GET FIRED'
PRESE

HR ... ED WAYS TO DEAL WITH IDIOTS

BY
BUSTER
GUTT

TO

FROM

MEETINGS

What You Really Want To Say:

COULD THIS HAVE NOT BEEN A FUCKING EMAIL!

HR Approved Alternative:

Could we summarize this in writing for efficiency?

MEETINGS

What You Really Want To Say:

PLEASE SHUT THE FUCK UP. WE ALL KNOW YOU LOVE YOUR OWN FUCKING VOICE.

HR Approved Alternative:

Could we hear from others who haven't spoken yet?

MEETINGS

What You Really Want To Say:

**FUCK ME!
I'VE AGED 10
YEARS IN THIS
MEETING.**

HR Approved Alternative:

That was thorough — maybe next time we can keep it concise.

MEETINGS

What You Really Want To Say:

YOUR POWERPOINT HAS WAY TOO MANY FUCKING SLIDES!

HR Approved Alternative:

That's very detailed — perhaps we could highlight the key points.

MEETINGS

What You Really Want To Say:

IF I HEAR 'CIRCLE BACK' AGAIN, I'LL WILL LEAVE THIS FUCKING ROOM!

HR Approved Alternative:

Maybe we can try a different phrase for clarity.

DEADLINES

What You Really Want To Say:

YOU HAD
ONE FUCKING JOB
AND YOU STILL
FUCKED IT UP!

HR Approved Alternative:

Let's revisit responsibilities to make sure we're aligned.

DEADLINES

What You Really Want To Say:

**YOUR
PROCRASTINATION IS
IS GETTING ON MY
FUCKING NERVES!**

HR Approved Alternative:

We should plan earlier
to avoid
last-minute stress.

DEADLINES

What You Really Want To Say:

WHY AM I NOT SURPRISED YOU MISSED THE FUCKING DEADLINE AGAIN.

HR Approved Alternative:

Let's discuss how we can better support you in meeting deadlines.

DEADLINES

What You Really Want To Say:

DO YOU EVEN OWN A FUCKING CALENDAR?

HR Approved Alternative:

Would reminders help keep things on track?

APPROVED

DEADLINES

What You Really Want To Say:

WHY CAN'T YOU MEET A FUCKING DEADLINE?

HR Approved Alternative:

Maybe we can clarify which deadlines are flexible and which are firm.

EMAILS

What You Really Want To Say:

YOUR EMAIL WAS SO LONG I FUCKING FELL ASLEEP!

HR Approved Alternative:

Could we keep emails more concise?

APPROVED

EMAILS

What You Really Want To Say:

DID YOU CC THE ENTIRE FUCKING PLANET?

HR Approved Alternative:

Maybe we can limit recipients to those directly involved.

EMAILS

What You Really Want To Say:

YOUR SHITTY EMAIL MADE ZERO FUCKING SENSE.

HR Approved Alternative:

Could you clarify a few points in your message?

EMAILS

What You Really Want To Say:

STOP REPLYING 'ALL' FOR FUCKS SAKE!

HR Approved Alternative:

Perhaps we can use direct replies to avoid inbox clutter.

APPROVED

EMAILS

What You Really Want To Say:

YOUR SUBJECT LINE WAS 'IMPORTANT' ... IT WAS A WASTE OF FUCKING TIME!

HR Approved Alternative:

Maybe we can use more specific subject lines.

OFFICE HABITS

What You Really Want To Say:

STOP FUCKING MICROWAVING FISH!

HR Approved Alternative:

Could we agree on less pungent lunch options?

OFFICE HABITS

What You Really Want To Say:

YOUR DESK LOOKS LIKE A FUCKING CRIME SCENE.

HR Approved Alternative:

Maybe we could tidy up for a more organized workspace.

APPROVED

OFFICE HABITS

What You Really Want To Say:

YOU TYPE LIKE A FUCKING PSYCHOPATH!

HR Approved Alternative:

Your typing is energetic — maybe a quieter keyboard would help.

OFFICE HABITS

What You Really Want To Say:

WHY THE FUCK ARE YOU ON SPEAKERPHONE?

HR Approved Alternative:

Could you use headphones to minimize background noise?

OFFICE HABITS

What You Really Want To Say:

WHY THE FUCK ARE YOU SO MESSY?

HR Approved Alternative:

Let's keep the space professional for everyone's comfort.

COFFEE & BREAKS

What You Really Want To Say:

YOU DRINK MORE FUCKING COFFEE THAN WATER.

HR Approved Alternative:

You really enjoy coffee — maybe we should stock more options.

COFFEE & BREAKS

What You Really Want To Say:

YOU TAKE FUCKING BREAKS LIKE IT'S A FULL-TIME JOB.

HR Approved Alternative:

“Let’s balance break times to keep productivity steady.

COFFEE & BREAKS

What You Really Want To Say:

YOU'RE ALWAYS 'JUST GRABBING A SNACK.' HOW ABOUT JUST DOING SOME FUCKING WORK!

HR Approved Alternative:

You seem to enjoy the kitchen — maybe we can set snack times.

COFFEE & BREAKS

What You Really Want To Say:

YOU TREAT THE VENDING MACHINE LIKE A FUCKING SOULMATE.

HR Approved Alternative:

You're a loyal customer — maybe we should rotate snack options.

COFFEE & BREAKS

What You Really Want To Say:

YOU DISAPPEAR FOR 'COFFEE' AND RETURN 45 MINUTES LATER.

WHAT THE FUCK!

HR Approved Alternative:

Could we keep breaks within the agreed timeframe?

TECH TROUBLES

What You Really Want To Say:

YOU FUCKING BREAK MORE COMPUTERS THAN HACKERS DO.

HR Approved Alternative:

Maybe IT can give extra training on troubleshooting.

TECH TROUBLES

What You Really Want To Say:

**FUCK ME!
YOU STILL DON'T
KNOW HOW TO
FUCKING MUTE
YOURSELF ON ZOOM?**

HR Approved Alternative:

Let's review Zoom basics
to avoid interruptions.

TECH TROUBLES

What You Really Want To Say:

YOUR SCREEN SHARING IS A FUCKING SHIT SHOW.

HR Approved Alternative:

Could we practice screen sharing before the meeting?

TECH TROUBLES

What You Really Want To Say:

YOU TREAT EXCEL LIKE FUCKING WITCHCRAFT.

HR Approved Alternative:

Would you like a quick Excel tutorial?

TECH TROUBLES

What You Really Want To Say:

YOU FUCKING CALL TECH SUPPORT MORE THAN YOUR FAMILY.

HR Approved Alternative:

Maybe we can empower you with some self-help guides.

TEAMWORK

What You Really Want To Say:

YOU'RE FUCKING ALLERGIC TO TEAMWORK.

HR Approved Alternative:

Let's find ways to collaborate more effectively.

TEAMWORK

What You Really Want To Say:

ISN'T IT INTERESTING HOW YOU VANISH WHEN THERE'S ACTUAL FUCKING WORK TO DO?

HR Approved Alternative:

Could we ensure everyone contributes equally?

APPROVED

TEAMWORK

What You Really Want To Say:

YOU TAKE CREDIT LIKE IT'S A FREE FUCKING SAMPLE.

HR Approved Alternative:

Let's acknowledge everyone's contributions fairly.

APPROVED

TEAMWORK

What You Really Want To Say:

YOU'RE THE SHITTY HUMAN VERSION OF 'BUFFERING.'

HR Approved Alternative:

Maybe we can streamline your workflow for speed.

APPROVED

TEAMWORK

What You Really Want To Say:

YOU'RE A FUCKING PROFESSIONAL MEETING DODGER.

HR Approved Alternative:

Could we schedule times that work better for you?

RANDOM ANNOYANCES

What You Really Want To Say:

PLEASE STOP HUMMING SO FUCKING LOUDLY.

HR Approved Alternative:

Could we keep noise levels low for focus?

RANDOM ANNOYANCES

What You Really Want To Say:

YOUR SHIT RINGTONE IS STUCK IN 2005.

HR Approved Alternative:

Maybe a quieter ringtone would be less distracting.

RANDOM ANNOYANCES

What You Really Want To Say:

YOU SNEEZE LIKE A FUCKING FOGHORN.

HR Approved Alternative:

Could we keep tissues handy for comfort?

RANDOM ANNOYANCES

What You Really Want To Say:

YOU TALK LOUDER THAN A FUCKING MEGAPHONE.

HR Approved Alternative:

Let’s keep voices at a moderate level.

BOSS INTERACTIONS

What You Really Want To Say:

YOU BROWN-NOSE LIKE IT'S A FUCKING SPORT.

HR Approved Alternative:

You're very supportive — maybe we can balance perspectives.

APPROVED

BOSS INTERACTIONS

What You Really Want To Say:

YOU LAUGH AT EVERY BOSS JOKE, EVEN THE SHIT ONES.

HR Approved Alternative:

You're very encouraging — maybe we can keep it natural.

BOSS INTERACTIONS

What You Really Want To Say:

WHY THE FUCK DO YOU VOLUNTEER US FOR THINGS WE DIDN'T AGREE TO?

HR Approved Alternative:

Could we confirm team consent before committing?

BOSS INTERACTIONS

What You Really Want To Say:

YOU TREAT THE BOSS LIKE A FUCKING CELEBRITY.

HR Approved Alternative:

You're very respectful — maybe we can keep it professional.

APPROVED

BOSS INTERACTIONS

What You Really Want To Say:

YOU NOD SO FUCKING MUCH, YOUR NECK MUST REALLY HURT.

HR Approved Alternative:

You're very agreeable — maybe we can add constructive feedback too.

PERSONAL QUIRKS

What You Really Want To Say:

YOU WEAR COLOGNE LIKE IT'S A FUCKING WEAPON.

HR Approved Alternative:

Could we keep scents subtle for shared spaces?

PERSONAL QUIRKS

What You Really Want To Say:

YOU TREAT CASUAL FRIDAY LIKE IT'S A FUCKING COSTUME PARTY.

HR Approved Alternative:

Let's keep casual Friday within professional limits.

PERSONAL QUIRKS

What You Really Want To Say:

YOU OVERSHARE LIKE IT'S A FUCKING THERAPY SESSION.

HR Approved Alternative:

Maybe we can keep conversations more work-focused.

PERSONAL QUIRKS

What You Really Want To Say:

STOP FUCKING SINGING! YOU TREAT THE OFFICE LIKE KARAOKE NIGHT.

HR Approved Alternative:

Could we save singing for after hours?

PERSONAL QUIRKS

What You Really Want To Say:

YOU'RE ALWAYS FUCKING LATE, BUT NEVER SORRY.

HR Approved Alternative:

Could we work on punctuality together?

APPROVED

FOOD & KITCHEN

What You Really Want To Say:

YOU LEAVE DIRTY DISHES LIKE IT'S A FUCKING PIECE OF ART!

HR Approved Alternative:

Could we clean up after ourselves in the kitchen?

FOOD & KITCHEN

What You Really Want To Say:

STOP EATING OTHER PEOPLE'S FUCKING LUNCH!

HR Approved Alternative:

Let's respect labeled food in the fridge.

FOOD & KITCHEN

What You Really Want To Say:

YOU TREAT THE FRIDGE LIKE A FUCKING SCIENCE EXPERIMENT.

HR Approved Alternative:

Could we clear expired items regularly?

APPROVED

FOOD & KITCHEN

What You Really Want To Say:

STOP HOGGING THE FUCKING COFFEE MACHINE.

HR Approved Alternative:

Let’s share the coffee machine fairly.

FOOD & KITCHEN

What You Really Want To Say:

WHY THE FUCK CAN'T YOU STOP SPILLING THE SUGAR EVERYWHERE?

HR Approved Alternative:

Could we keep the kitchen tidy for everyone?

DRESS CODE

What You Really Want To Say:

YOUR TIE LOOKS LIKE IT'S FROM A FUCKING CLOWN SHOP.

HR Approved Alternative:

That's bold — maybe a simpler style would fit better.

APPROVED

DRESS CODE

What You Really Want To Say:

WHY THE FUCK ARE YOU WEARING FLIP-FLOPS TO WORK?

HR Approved Alternative:

Could we keep footwear professional?

DRESS CODE

What You Really Want To Say:

YOUR FUCKING SHIRT IS LOUDER THAN YOUR FUCKING VOICE.

HR Approved Alternative:

That’s colorful — maybe tone it down for meetings.

APPROVED

DRESS CODE

What You Really Want To Say:

YOU TREAT MY SHIT LIKE IT'S YOUR FUCKING SHIT!

HR Approved Alternative:

Let's make sure we return anything we borrow.

DRESS CODE

What You Really Want To Say:

WHY THE FUCK ARE YOU WEARING SUNGLASSES INDOORS?

HR Approved Alternative:

Could we save those for outside?

APPROVED

TIME MANAGEMENT

What You Really Want To Say:

YOU'RE LATE TO EVERYTHING. EVERY FUCKING THING!

HR Approved Alternative:

Could we work on punctuality together?

TIME MANAGEMENT

What You Really Want To Say:

YOU LEAVE EARLY EVERY FUCKING DAY!

HR Approved Alternative:

Let's balance schedules fairly.

APPROVED

TIME MANAGEMENT

What You Really Want To Say:

YOU TAKE FUCKING FOREVER TO FINISH TASKS.

HR Approved Alternative:

Maybe we can streamline your workflow.

TIME MANAGEMENT

What You Really Want To Say:

YOU'RE ALWAYS FUCKING 'BUSY' BUT NEVER PRODUCTIVE.

HR Approved Alternative:

Could we prioritize tasks more effectively?

TIME MANAGEMENT

What You Really Want To Say:

YOU TREAT DEADLINES LIKE FUCKING BEDTIME STORIES.

HR Approved Alternative:

Let's clarify expectations around deadlines.

COMMUNICATION

What You Really Want To Say:

YOU TALK IN FUCKING RIDDLES.

HR Approved Alternative:

Could you explain that more clearly?

APPROVED

COMMUNICATION

What You Really Want To Say:

YOU FUCKING USE JARGON LIKE IT'S CONFETTI.

HR Approved Alternative:

Maybe we can simplify the language for clarity.

COMMUNICATION

What You Really Want To Say:

WHY DO YOU INTERRUPT CONSTANTLY, FOR FUCKS SAKE?

HR Approved Alternative:

Could we let others finish before jumping in?

COMMUNICATION

What You Really Want To Say:

YOU ENDLESSLY REPEAT YOURSELF OVER AND FUCKING OVER AGAIN!

HR Approved Alternative:

That's important — maybe we can summarize once.

COMMUNICATION

What You Really Want To Say:

YOU MUMBLE LIKE A FUCKING SECRET AGENT.

HR Approved Alternative:

Could you speak a bit louder for clarity?

APPROVED

WORKLOAD

What You Really Want To Say:

YOU DUMP TASKS LIKE YOU'RE FUCKING SANTA CLAUS!

HR Approved Alternative:

Could we balance workloads more evenly?

APPROVED

WORKLOAD

What You Really Want To Say:

WHERE THE FUCK DO YOU DISAPPEAR TO, WHEN THINGS GET TOUGH?

HR Approved Alternative:

Let's support each other during busy times.

WORKLOAD

What You Really Want To Say:

YOU TREAT DELEGATION LIKE A FUCKING HOBBY.

HR Approved Alternative:

Could we share responsibilities fairly?

WORKLOAD

What You Really Want To Say:

YOU AVOID RESPONSIBILITY LIKE IT'S FUCKING CONTAGIOUS.

HR Approved Alternative:

Let's clarify roles to ensure accountability.

WORKLOAD

What You Really Want To Say:

YOU TREAT DEADLINES LIKE THEY'RE FUCKING OPTIONAL.

HR Approved Alternative:

Maybe we can reinforce which ones are critical."

ATTITUDE

What You Really Want To Say:

YOU FUCKING COMPLAIN MORE THAN A TODDLER.

HR Approved Alternative:

Could we focus on solutions instead of problems?

ATTITUDE

What You Really Want To Say:

YOU'RE ALWAYS SO FUCKING NEGATIVE.

HR Approved Alternative:

Let's try to keep discussions constructive.

ATTITUDE

What You Really Want To Say:

YOU ACT LIKE YOU'RE THE FUCKING BOSS!

HR Approved Alternative:

Could we keep roles clear and collaborative?

ATTITUDE

What You Really Want To Say:

YOU'RE SO FUCKING DRAMATIC ABOUT EVERYTHING.

HR Approved Alternative:

Let's keep discussions calm and solution-focused.

ATTITUDE

What You Really Want To Say:

YOU ACT LIKE THE OFFICE IS YOUR FUCKING STAGE!

HR Approved Alternative:

You bring energy — maybe we can channel it into projects.

ATTITUDE

What You Really Want To Say:

YOU FUCKING ROLL YOUR EYES MORE THAN A TEENAGER!

HR Approved Alternative:

Could we keep reactions professional?

ATTITUDE

What You Really Want To Say:

YOU SIGH LOUDER THAN THE FUCKING PRINTER!

HR Approved Alternative:

Let’s keep frustrations low-key to maintain focus.

ATTITUDE

What You Really Want To Say:

YOU FUCKING COMPLAIN SO MUCH...IT'S LIKE YOUR SIDE HUSTLE.

HR Approved Alternative:

Could we frame challenges as opportunities?

ATTITUDE

What You Really Want To Say:

YOU TREAT FEEDBACK LIKE A IT'S A FUCKING PERSONAL ATTACK.

HR Approved Alternative:

Let's see feedback as a growth tool.

ATTITUDE

What You Really Want To Say:

YOU'RE FUCKING ALLERGIC TO POSITIVITY.

HR Approved Alternative:

Could we try to highlight wins more often?

PRODUCTIVITY

What You Really Want To Say:

YOU WORK SLOWER THAN FUCKING DIAL-UP INTERNET.

HR Approved Alternative:

Maybe we can streamline your workflow.

PRODUCTIVITY

What You Really Want To Say:

YOU MULTITASK LIKE A FUCKING BROKEN ROBOT.

HR Approved Alternative:

Let's focus on one task at a time for efficiency.

PRODUCTIVITY

What You Really Want To Say:

YOU SPEND MORE TIME CHATTING THAN GETTING SHIT DONE.

HR Approved Alternative:

Could we balance social time with productivity?

APPROVED

PRODUCTIVITY

What You Really Want To Say:

YOU TREAT DEADLINES LIKE THEY'RE FUCKING SPEED BUMPS.

HR Approved Alternative:

Let's keep momentum steady to meet goals.

PRODUCTIVITY

What You Really Want To Say:

YOU'RE ALWAYS SO FUCKING BUSY BUT NEVER EFFECTIVE.

HR Approved Alternative:

Could we prioritize tasks for better outcomes?

HUMOR

What You Really Want To Say:

YOUR SHIT JOKES ARE OLDER THAN THE FUCKING OFFICE FURNITURE.

HR Approved Alternative:

You bring humor — maybe we can keep it fresh.

HUMOR

What You Really Want To Say:

YOUR FUCKING STORIES ARE LONGER THAN A NETFLIX SERIES!

HR Approved Alternative:

Could we keep anecdotes short and sweet?

HUMOR

What You Really Want To Say:

YOU THINK YOU'RE THE FUCKING OFFICE COMEDIAN!

HR Approved Alternative:

You lighten the mood — maybe we can balance it with focus.

HUMOR

What You Really Want To Say:

YOUR SARCASM COULD POWER THE FUCKING BUILDING.

HR Approved Alternative:

Could we keep tone constructive for clarity?

MISCELLANEOUS

What You Really Want To Say:

YOU TREAT THE PRINTER LIKE IT'S YOUR FUCKING ENEMY.

HR Approved Alternative:

Maybe we can get IT to check the printer.

MISCELLANEOUS

What You Really Want To Say:

YOU HOARD OFFICE SUPPLIES LIKE IT'S FUCKING TREASURE.

HR Approved Alternative:

Could we share supplies fairly among the team?

APPROVED

MISCELLANEOUS

What You Really Want To Say:

YOU TREAT THE THERMOSTAT LIKE IT'S A FUCKING PERSONAL TOY.

HR Approved Alternative:

Let's agree on a comfortable temperature for everyone.

MISCELLANEOUS

What You Really Want To Say:

YOU GOSSIP MORE THAN A FUCKING SOAP OPERA.

HR Approved Alternative:

Could we keep conversations work-related?

MISCELLANEOUS

What You Really Want To Say:

YOU ACT LIKE HR IS YOUR OWN PRIVATE FUCKING BABYSITTER.

HR Approved Alternative:

Let's take ownership of our professionalism.

APPROVED

MISCELLANEOUS

What You Really Want To Say:

YOUR EXCEL SKILLS ARE SO BAD, EVEN CLIPPY FUCKING QUIT.

HR Approved Alternative:

Maybe we can schedule a quick Excel refresher.

MISCELLANEOUS

What You Really Want To Say:

YOU TREAT DEADLINES LIKE NETFLIX RECOMMENDATIONS — FUCKING OPTIONAL.

HR Approved Alternative:

Let’s clarify which deadlines are flexible and which are firm.

MISCELLANEOUS

What You Really Want To Say:

YOUR POWERPOINT TRANSITIONS FUCKING GAVE ME MOTION SICKNESS.

HR Approved Alternative:

Could we simplify the slide transitions for clarity?

APPROVED

MISCELLANEOUS

What You Really Want To Say:

YOU TAKE COFFEE BREAKS LIKE YOU'RE TRAINING FOR A FUCKING MARATHON.

HR Approved Alternative:

Could we keep breaks within the agreed timeframe?

MISCELLANEOUS

What You Really Want To Say:

YOU'RE FUCKING LATE SO OFTEN, WE SHOULD START MEETINGS IN A DIFFERENT TIME ZONE.

HR Approved Alternative:

Could we work on punctuality together?

Printed in Dunstable, United Kingdom

74829673R00061